JUST PRETEND

A Freethought Book for Children

By Dan Barker
Illustrated by Alma Cuebas

Freedom From Religion Foundation, Inc.
PO Box 750, Madison WI 53701

For Becky, Kristi, Andrea, and Danny.
And Pacal.

Published by the Freedom From Religion Foundation, Inc., PO Box 750, Madison, Wisconsin, 53701.

FFRF, Inc. Web Site: http://www.ffrf.org

First edition, September 1988.
Second edition, August 2002.

ISBN 1-877733-05-9

There is no one in the world who is exactly like you.

You are a human being and you have a mind of your own.

Your mind is very special.

Your mind helps you to know what is true and false.

If someone told you there is a million dollars in the back of
   this book, would you believe it?

Probably not. And just to be sure, you could look.

There's not a million dollars in this book. And you can use
   your mind to prove it.

It's sometimes fun to pretend.

Most of us like to hear stories, or imagine things that are not true.

Stories can make us laugh or cry.

They can make us feel happy or brave.

They sometimes help us to feel special.

But sometimes people really believe stories that are JUST
  PRETEND.

A myth is a story that some people think is true, but it is really
  JUST PRETEND.

For example, Zeus, the lightning god, is a myth.
And the Easter Bunny is a myth.

And so is the Tooth Fairy, Frankenstein, Leprechauns, Mother
  Goose, Jack and the Beanstalk, Humpty Dumpty, The
  Bogeyman, Paul Bunyan, and many other stories.

How do you know these stories are not true?

Because you use your mind. You think about it, and you see
  there is no proof. They are just stories.

They are JUST PRETEND.

Many people believe in Santa Claus.

It is a very nice story.

But when you get older, you learn that Santa Claus is not real.

Some kids feel sad when they learn that Santa Claus is a myth.

But some kids say they thought it was JUST PRETEND all
along.

Most kids are glad to grow up and learn the truth.

Why do so many children believe in Santa Claus?

Because when they were very young they were told that Santa is real.

Children believe Santa is real because they enjoy the story.

It's fun to think of gifts, elves, reindeer, and a jolly old man with a red suit who lives at the North Pole and secretly brings gifts into your house at night.

Some children believe in Santa because it makes them think about being good.

Adults sometimes tell children they should be good or Santa may not bring any presents.

They think Santa is watching them all year, making a list, and checking it twice.

Many children believe in Santa because they see things that
  seem to prove Santa is real.

They see presents under the Christmas tree.

They see stockings stuffed
with goodies.

Sometimes Santa's midnight
snack disappears.

Sometimes they get the very
gift they asked for.

Children believe in Santa because many people talk about
Santa.

They hear Santa songs on the TV and radio.

They hear about Santa from books and records.

They see Santa on cards and at stores.

Children believe in Santa because no one seems to question if Santa is real.

Not at school.

Not at church.

Not at home.

How do we know that the Santa story is just a myth?

If you use your mind, you can think why.

One of the reasons Santa is JUST PRETEND is because no one has ever seen the real Santa.

No one has ever taken his picture.

The Santas that you see in stores and at parties are just fake Santas. They are people who dress up like Santa every year because they want children to have fun—and they sometimes want to sell toys.

Another reason we know Santa is not true is because there is nothing but ice and snow at the North Pole.

And reindeer can't fly.

How could Santa know what every kid wants for Christmas?

No one can read minds, especially not billions of minds all over
the world.

And a fat old man couldn't fit through most chimneys.

Ant think about this: There are billions of children in the world.

In order to get to every home in the world on Christmas Eve, Santa would have to visit about 10,000 homes every second!

Think about it. He wouldn't have time to go back and reload his sleigh.

He would have to carry over a billion presents at once!

If you think about it, it is easy to see that Santa Claus is a myth.

It is a fun story that makes many people feel happy every year.

But you can still be happy, even if there is no Santa.

And you can JUST PRETEND that Santa is real, just for fun.

That's what most grownups do.

Do you know that many people believe in God?

They think God made the world and runs the universe.

Some people grow up and learn that God is JUST PRETEND,
  like Santa.

But some people still believe God is real.

Some people think God is a man.

Some people think God is a woman.

Some people think God is an animal.

Some people think God is part animal and part human.

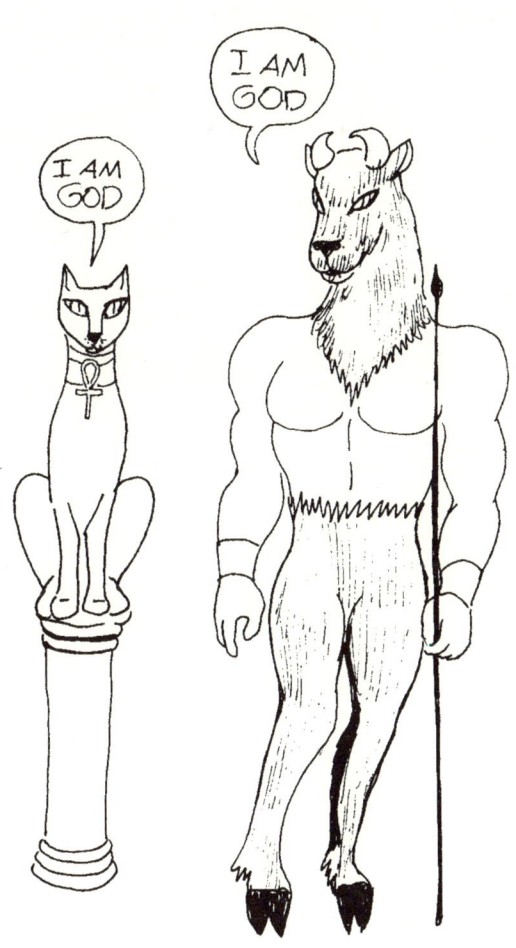

Some people think there are many gods.

Some people think God is just nature.

They think they see God in flowers, birds, mountains, sunshine, and lightning.

Some people believe in a god you can touch.

Some people believe in a god who is a ghost.

Some people believe in a god who gives rewards to favorite people.

They imagine a place called Heaven with gold and crowns and music and no pain or work.

Some people believe in a god who burns people who are bad.
They imagine a place called Hell with fire and pain and
  screams.

They think God hates people who don't think the same way as
  they do.

Some people think God is a Christian.

Some people think God is a Moslem.

Or a Jew.

Or a Catholic.

Or a Baptist.

They way people think about God is called religion.

There are thousands of different religions.

If you think about it, they can't all be right.

Somebody must be wrong.

Maybe they are all wrong!

Why do so many people believe in a god?

It's just like the Santa Claus myth.

People believe in a god because they were told God is real.

Most people were told about a god when they were young
   children.

People usually believe in the religion in which they were born.

If you were born in a Moslem country, you will probably grow up to be Moslem.

If you were born into a Jewish family, you will probably grow up to believe in Judaism.

If you were born in a Christian community, you will probably grow up to believe in Jesus.

Many people believe in a god because they like the story.

They like to think about angels.

They like to imagine things that happened long ago or far away.

They like the stories of adventure, battles and wars—such as
the story in the bible about how David killed a giant.

They enjoy hearing about talking animals and evil demons.

They like to think about impossible miracles.

Many people believe in a god because it makes them think about being good. Like Santa Claus.

They think God will take care of them.

They think God will make good things happen to them if they are good.

They think God will punish all the bad people in the world.

They think God lets bad things happen to bad people.

They think that no one can ever get away with doing bad things, like crime. They hope God will punish criminals forever.

Many people believe in a god because they see things that
  seem to prove God is real.

Sometimes lucky things happen to them.

Sometimes sickness goes away.

Sometimes they pray for things, and they get what they pray for.

Some people think they hear a god talking to them in their minds.

Some people dream about a god and they think it is real.

People believe in God because other people are always talking about God.

Ministers, priests, rabbis, and other religious leaders talk about God a lot!

There are many songs about God.

There are many movies, plays, books, cards and pictures about God.

There are churches, synagogues, mosques, and temples all over the world. Some people think their God lives in these buildings.

Many people believe in God because no one seems to question if God is real.

Not at school.

Not at church.

Not at home.

Some people say it is not nice to question God.

They think that believing the myth is more important than
  finding out what is really true.

Some people believe in God for a long time.

They have never changed their minds since they were little children.

But some people do not believe in God.

They are called ATHEISTS.

They are sometimes called AGNOSTICS or FREETHINKERS.

Some of them used to believe in God when they were young.

But some atheists never believed in God at all.

Some people feel sad when they learn that God is just a myth.

Some people say they knew it was JUST PRETEND all along.

They know that every baby is born an atheist.

They know that if you are never told you must believe in a god, you will stay an atheist all your life.

Why do some people not believe in God?

If you use your mind, you can think why.

Like Santa Claus, no one has ever seen God.

No one has ever taken God's picture.

Another reason people think God is JUST PRETEND is because there is nothing in outer space except planets, stars, galaxies and stuff.

No one has ever found Heaven, or God, or angels. They are not real.

And no one has ever found a dark world under the ground
where demons live.

The earth is a globe made of rock with a melted center.

Heaven and Hell are JUST PRETEND.

Some people do not believe in God because they know that religious stories can't really happen in real life.

Everyone knows that snakes don't talk. Donkeys don't speak human language.

People don't walk on water or float in the air by themselves.

But the Bible says all these things happened, so the Bible can't be true, can it?

Mountains don't fly, and sticks do not turn into snakes.

And scientists know that a woman did not come from a man's rib.

That is silly.

Think about it.

Noah's Ark can't be true because there is not enough water to cover the highest mountains.

How could Noah get all those animals on the boat?

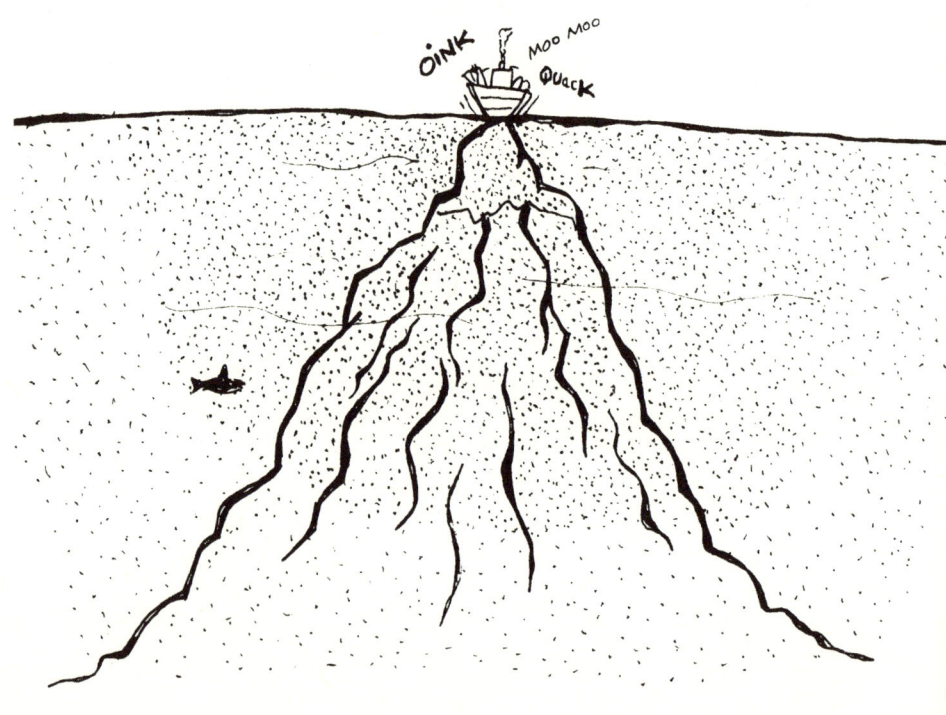

Were there two of each kind of dinosaur? Two penguins? Two of each of millions of different kinds of beetles, cockroaches, rattlesnakes, vultures, and bedbugs?

There would not be enough room on the Ark for millions of animals to live for so many months.

Some animals eat other animals. How could Noah keep them from eating each other?

Some people find it hard to believe that Jonah could live for three days in the stomach of a fish.

Or that Buddha was born speaking.

Or that evil comes from Pandora's little box.

Or that the Nile River was turned to blood.

Or that Shadrach, Meshach and Abednego could live in a hot furnace without protection.

Or that Joshua could make the sun stand still.

Do you think these things really happened?

And think about this:

There are billions of people in the world.

To pay attention to everyone, God would have to listen to
  more than 10,000 prayers every second!

Do you think anyone could really do that?

Do you really think there is some big brain up in outer space
that can do all that?

Do you think someone could be everywhere at once?

Many years ago people didn't know very much, so they invented gods to answer their questions.

Some people don't believe in God because they learn that the stories about God are just made up, like Santa Claus.

They learn that the Bible, the Koran, and the Vedas are filled with mistakes and wild stories.

They were written by people who thought it was true.

But it was really JUST PRETEND.

Most religions teach that God is good.

But then why is there so much pain in the world?

Why is there ugliness and unfairness?

If there is a good God, why does he let people suffer? Why is there cancer and murder and tornadoes and poisonous spiders?

And if God is good, why does the bible show God doing so
many terrible things?

In the bible, God starts wars and murders people. He drowned
millions of people in a flood. Is that nice?

There are many other bad stories in the bible.

God made two bears come out of the forest and kill 42 children.

And he made women less important than men.

And he made the earth open up and swallow some people.

Do you think these things are nice?

Do you think these things really happened?

Most children think Jesus was a man of love.

But he also told people to cut off their hands and pluck out
their eyes.

And Jesus said we should hate our parents.

The bible says he drowned 2,000 pigs!

And he believed
in a hot hell
where God will
burn people
who do not
think the same
way he
thought.

Is that nice? Do you believe that?

Most religions teach that you can't be a good person if you don't believe in God.

But many atheists and agnostics are good people.

And although some religious persons are kind, some are not.

It's not what you think that makes you good or bad.

It's what you do that makes you good or bad.

Most religions have caused some very bad things.

Their followers have started wars.

They have owned slaves and killed people who believed in different religions.

Some of them teach that it is okay to hurt children, and that men are better than women.

Some of them teach that light-skinned people are better than dark-skinned people.

Some people notice that prayers are never answered.

Once in a while people think prayers are answered, but it is usually something that would have happened anyway, or something that a person made happen.

And sometimes people JUST PRETEND that their prayers have been answered.

Have you ever prayed for something that didn't happen?

The bible says that God will give you whatever you ask for. But we all know that prayer doesn't work.

And no one has ever found proof that there is life after death.

Everyone who finally dies, stays dead.

Some people dream about dead people, but that doesn't mean
   they are still alive, does it?

Atheists know that even though many people believe in God, it is just a myth, because it can't be proved.

It is just like Santa Claus.

If you could prove God, then there would be no atheists.

Think about it.

And think about this:

If God made everything, then who made God?

No one can tell you what to think.

Not your teachers.

Not your parents.

Not your minister, priest, or rabbi.

Not your friends or relatives.

Not this book.

You are the boss of your own mind.

If you have used your mind to find out what is true, then you should be proud!

Your thoughts are free.

If you are an atheist, then you know that

God Is Just Pretend.

Message to Parents

Every day children in North America are exposed to religious indoctrination, especially Christianity. Even children in nonreligious households hear about "God," "Jesus," and "the bible" at an early age. It's inevitable!

Learning about religious beliefs around the world and across the centuries can be useful. An educated child necessarily must be exposed to differing beliefs about religion— including freethought. However, an unbalanced treatment of religion can be unhealthy for a child's development.

For an understanding of religion, it is important to know about the bible (all of it: the good and the bad). But it is also important to know about the Koran, the Vedas, the Book of Mormon, and other scriptures. A child who is exclusively exposed to one point of view is apt to consider any other religious belief as foreign and threatening to the "one true faith." That child may grow up to perpetuate the intolerances of the past.

Child developmentalists like Piaget have shown that children grow through stages. It is only around the age of 12 that a person is ready to handle abstracts. To expose young children to ideas like substitutionary atonement, original sin, or the trinity (concepts that adults can't really comprehend) is confusing and even harmful. Psychologists at Living Skills Press, a publisher of educational materials, remind us that the bible is written by adults for adults, and was never intended to be used directly with children. The bible should be rated 'R'—for every reason that a movie is rated 'R': adult themes, violence, sex and language.

Just Pretend provides children with another way of thinking about religion. Freethought—the formation of opinions about religion on the basis of reason rather than faith or authority—is a respectable position with a rich heritage. Freethinkers do not believe in brainwashing children, but in encouraging children to think for themselves and, if necessary, to question authority. Wise parents will allow children to make their own decision, or no decision, in their own time and in their own way. Children should not be expected to make any final decision about religion until they are adults. The most important message of *Just Pretend* is to remind the child that no other person can control his or her own thoughts.

Dan Barker

The Freedom From Religion Foundation is a national freethought organization founded in 1978 to help protect the American principle of state/church separation and to educate the public about the views of nontheists.

Freedom From Religion Foundation, Inc.
PO Box 750 • Madison WI 53701 • www.ffrf.org